THE JHENNA

How to Beat PTSD and Find Peace

Damon Dusang

NEWMAN SPRINGS PUBLISHING
320 Broad Street
Red Bank, NJ 07701

First originally published by Newman
Springs Publishing 2024

ISBN 979-8-89308-747-5 (Paperback)
ISBN 979-8-89308-748-2 (Digital)

Printed in the United States of America

This book is dedicated to Jhenna. She saved my life and gave me a chance at a better one. I will always be grateful for her in my life. She is everything; I'm nothing. It's in that nothingness that I found peace. In that that peace, I found the strength to be better, to stand tall, to hold my head high, to not be ashamed, to write *The Jhenna.*

She's my hero. She's my friend. She's extremely important to me.

> Don't worry so much. Everything is fine, and you're doing well. Keep looking toward a happy future and manifest the happiness you seek. It will come. (Jhenna)

PART 1

Introduction

I live on the Mississippi Gulf Coast and have relatives in New Orleans, Louisiana. I was approached. "Damon, we have a bank job and need your skill set. You've been in the army for a minute, and we need you on the job."

I didn't want to be a bank robber when I was born, but I knew I had to do something with my life, and I wanted to be needed. So I asked, "What do you need me to do?"

They said, "Fill this out."

I thought, *An application to be a bank robber? This is stupid.*

First blank, "Date." Answer, "No, I'm married."

Next blank, "Name." Answer, "My wife's name is not your business."

Next blank, "Sex." Answer, "Not enough! But that ain't your business either!"

Needless to say, I couldn't even get a job as a bank robber. Thank you, PTSD! Then the following happened.

If you have served more than 2.5 seconds in the Army, you know that if the boss says, "You can either voluntarily get a mental health evaluation, or if this behavior continues, it will be command mandated," you know you are going to get a mental health evaluation. The question is, will it be sooner or later? That is what happened to me in December of 2021. I received a counseling statement describing my behavior. The list was long: sporadic behavior; messages of love, anger, sadness, anxiety, and paranoia. I chose to voluntarily get the evaluation, yet I was so far down the rabbit hole of PTSD that I couldn't make my own appointment and told the commanding officer (CO). For him to make the appointment for me, he had to make it command mandated, and my medical records now show it was command mandated. My anger turned to rage when I learned of this. Still, I was a lucky one. I had strong leadership. I had a first sergeant (1SG), and I trusted her completely.

I had been in therapy for a year prior to that date with a civilian whose only concern was to get me into marriage counseling. The problem was me, not my wife. Things were getting worse, and I finally snapped when I lost a Soldier whom I called a friend. My first loss in my military career of over twenty years of service that spanned a time frame of more than five decades, with breaks in service. After December 2021, I began seeing military psychologists and care providers. I was on medications that I couldn't stand taking. I was even on sleeping medications that caused me twice to strike out in my sleep. The first time, I punched my wife in my sleep, and thankfully, she screamed, which woke me. The second time, I punched a picture that was on my nightstand, shattering the glass and knocking everything off that nightstand. That's when I stopped taking all medications and started looking for a way to beat PTSD. I refused to live my life that way.

It was then, while going to my mental health treatments with psychologists and other professionals, that I realized it was not enough. It didn't work fast enough. I didn't seem to make progress. I had to find answers fast. Although I still attend mental health appointments, three times a week in the beginning, now every two weeks, I use the techniques in this book to go from being angry all the time to sometimes getting over anger in less than ten minutes. I still have bad days, and I still get angry. I do find peace most days. That is a wonderful feeling.

The benefit of this, "the Jhenna", is that the tools work. Not everything will fit your needs, but you will find powerful techniques that will keep you at peace most of the time. It is not something you do once, and you're fixed. There is no cure for PTSD, my doctor told me on my second appointment when I asked, "How do we fix this?" However, PTSD can be beaten. Jhenna once told me, "If you get mental health treatment, you'll have a chance to be happy, a chance to have friends, a chance to be loved." I believed her, and she was right. I have all of that now. You can too.

PART 2

What PTSD Does

In this section, you'll find the things Jhenna said to me, and I'll explain the process that I had to go through to understand what she was talking about. When you have PTSD, as well as when you are angry, you don't think right, or maybe you just don't understand simple things. It's a process rewiring our brains.

"Don't dwell on it. Don't overthink it. Don't think too much into it."

To me, this was the same as saying "Don't think about a pink elephant," at the time. That was no help at all. But as I said, I trusted her. I believed that she wouldn't say something that wasn't meant to help me.

I started asking myself, "How do you not think about something that has you completely overwhelmed or angry in the moment?" After my mental health session, I would spend anywhere from eight hours to sometimes days searching for an answer so that I didn't "dwell on it, overthink it, or think too much into it" After all, I wasn't sleeping, and I couldn't turn it off, which made it worse, so I would search harder. Even when I found something, I was still thinking about what she told me not to "dwell on." Book after book, I read on meditation, Zen, finding peace, mindfulness, etc. I used the techniques that the doctors gave me. One was just to imagine putting that thought on a leaf and watching it float away down a river. I was too anxious to do that, although I tried many times, and it seemed to make matters so bad that I couldn't catch my breath.

"Take a breath."

That is not a great one for me when I am beyond anger and in rage during a face-to-face. However, Jhenna is smart. That one she only put in text messages. In a text message, it gave me more time without getting angrier, and I could breathe for a while and slowly let go of the anger. In the early days of treatment, I sent probably ten to twenty texts a day to Jhenna, and I know it had to be frustrating her. I was hurting so bad I just wanted some relief. I really hated life. I didn't mean to do that, and I certainly never asked for PTSD. I couldn't control myself. Jhenna was patient, kind, and, when needed, firm. It took me trusting her and her patience with me to make this work. It was hard on both of us. After all, dealing with a crazy person can't be easy.

"Settle down" or "Please settle down."

Of all the things that Jhenna would say to me, this one worked the best in person. She had a certain look on her face when she said it. Later, she would just give the look, and I knew I needed to settle down. It wasn't *that* look a parent gives when the child is about two seconds from being in big trouble. "Settle down" is gentle, as opposed to "Calm down." "Calm down" is used so many times in banks, department stores, restaurants, and even on television and movies. I've never seen it work. In the movies or television, the scene is usually the same: a male and a female, usually in a heated argument, voices raised, when the male usually shouts over the top of the female, who is very upset and shouting, "Calm down!" The female usually responds with, "Calm down? Don't tell me to calm down!" thus the argument continues.

This reminds me of the times I had arguments with my wife, and she was not even present! An argument in my head that is very heated, and by the time she gets home, the air is so thick with tension that she knows something is wrong, and the argument begins. I'm sure that's never happened to anyone else before. Although I saw it in a comedy where the comedian explained the very thing: the husband comes home, she goes off on him, he looks confused and has no idea what's going on, and it's because he wasn't part of the two-hour argument she had in her head before he got home, and she picked up in the middle of the argument, and all he can say is, "What are you talking about?" That's never fun. "Settle down" sounds so much nicer and always settled me down very fast.

This is perhaps a tip for those of you living with or loving a person with PTSD. As I remember, when Jhenna said that to me with the look that went with it, I'd get quiet and take a breath. That's a bonus. Above, I mentioned that Jhenna never told me to "take a breath" face-to-face. She'd say, "Settle down.

Please settle down. I'd want you to settle down," thus ending my tantrum.

"Be sure to give yourself credit. You did all the hard work."

This reminds me of the saying, "Don't break your arm patting yourself on the back." In my early days of mental health, it seemed a bit strange to me. It also reminds me of "Give me some credit! Gosh!" That's usually followed by something along the lines of "I'm not stupid, you know?" I find it funny looking back. It's a positive statement and maybe even a compliment. I don't ever remember anyone ever saying that to me before. It was only a short time ago that it meant you did a good job. So many folks that I speak to are trying to get their friends and loved ones to mental health treatment and haven't been able. My wife tried for nearly a decade. The point is, sometimes the words we say are not received in the way we intended them to be received. The receiver doesn't ask for clarification, and none is offered. Texting has almost eliminated one of the four things it takes to communicate.

I was taught (when being trained as a radio repairman at Fort Gordon, Georgia) that communication requires four things, or there is no communication. You must have a sender, someone transmitting the message. You must have a medium through which the message is sent—airwaves, sign language, hand signals. You must have a receiver, the person the message is intended for. And then the overlooked part in a message is often feedback.

I have completely overlooked the other parts of communication, such as tonality, body language, and facial expressions. Without feedback, I "think too much into things." I have to guess the meaning of what it means to give yourself credit. I was taught that after a job well done, you have a beer. That's giving yourself credit. I did a lot of that. I mistook a compliment for having a beer. I had to change the way I think. I am in mental health treatment for that very reason. Does that sound silly? Absolutely. Would we need mental health treatment if we all thought the same way? I don't have an answer for that. Do you? This kept me going to mental health treatment so that I could learn why someone tells you to have a beer and stop drinking. This caused me to really work hard to figure out what this meant. I knew that Jhenna was trying to help and be helpful, and I trusted her. Often in the military, we don't give ourselves credit because we are taught that we are just doing our jobs. We are supposed to do a good job. It's our job to do the best job that we can without expecting anything in return. When credit was given to us, it was by someone else, either a certificate or medal or a round of applause.

So why would she say, "Give yourself credit?" My opinion and what I accept to be true is that she was giving recognition just using different words. Words that I never heard before. A foreign language to me. Confusion often causes me frustration, and frustration leads to anger. At least for me. Nearly two years to figure that out. You can say, "Why didn't you just ask?" Why would I ask if I thought I knew what it meant? If you just finished mowing the lawn and the heat index is super high, down south in my circle, the statement, "You finished mowing the lawn in that heat? You should give yourself some credit!" means grab a cold one (cold beer). And I did! Which leads to a whole lot more. I have been told to think before I speak or think before I act. In the mental health treatment and dealing with PTSD, I learned that I definitely don't think the way everyone or many others do. How could I? My brain is wired wrong.

I believe that the trust I had for her was one of the most important factors that kept me going. Loved ones and close friends probably think a lot alike in many ways. Jhenna and I didn't grow up together, so we speak differently. A friend of mine (who used to be my professor at the Defense Language Institute, or DLI) would get onto me for referring to my baby as my baby and say I should refer to her as my daughter. She's already graduated college and is working, and I still refer to her as my baby, and I haven't ever called her by her correct name when I talk to her. Yet everyone knows who I am referring to when I call her "Angel." We spent over two decades together.

I do remember the first time moving down south, and I met one of my uncles, who asked me to bring him a can of "earl." He told me where to find it, and when I told him I couldn't see any, he told me I was looking right at it. He came and showed me. I said, "Oh, a can of oil?" He said, "That's what I said!"

An army example to a brand-new Soldier, maybe six months in service, who is often sent to supply to get two cans of backblast. *Backblast* is the blast that comes out of the rear of a shoulder-held rocket launcher. When firing, we are supposed to check the backblast area because anyone behind you will have about ten feet of fire and intense heat cook him.

I think the navy used to say to new folks on the submarine, "Go make sure the screen doors on the sub are closed. We don't need any fish getting in here."

The point here, I think, is you are going to have to have a common language to communicate effectively, and then I hope it'll be easier to help those get the help they need. You can't assume you have a common language even if you grew up together. One friend can tell a person, "Get lost!" using curse words, yet a new friend, not so much. And you always must be paying attention and adjusting your language or words to show support to a sensitive person. If you think they need help, they are going to be very sensitive for a while or emotional, if that word works better for you. It's hard having PTSD, and knowing what I've done in my early days of treatment, I know it's hard on the folks that care about us, maybe even harder. You have to be stronger and more patient than you may ever have been to help someone with PTSD. Jhenna was that for me. I was so messed up and started so many shitstorms that my CO at the time said to me, "You are disrupting the good order and discipline of the unit." I used to be a good Soldier. I didn't know what I was doing. That crushed me, and I remember the thought that came into my head, *Fuck this shit. I'm done.* It was an angry thought. I trusted him as well, and he worked hard to help me. I said, "I don't mean to. I'm working hard to get better." He knew I was and had to be firm at that time.

"Be open and honest."

This was a bit embarrassing for me. Once diagnosed, I was not allowed to handle weapons, go to the firing range, or participate in any combat-related training, which basically meant I wasn't a Soldier anymore to me. All the stuff I loved was taken away from me. They wouldn't even let me drive the bus, which I always looked forward to doing. The day we were to head out to the range is when I found out this information. To make it worse, I found out from the training NCO as I was drawing my weapon. I was asked by a Soldier to help with her weapon, and I always helped anyone who asked. If I couldn't personally help them because it required a different skill set or computer access, I knew where they needed to go and walked them there. This Soldier was the first I was open and honest with in the unit. I couldn't touch her weapon. I couldn't help her. I found someone to help her; it was the best I could do. She was only a year older than my daughter. I told her I was in treatment for mental health and not allowed to touch weapons. She told me I was brave for doing that and if there was anything she could do to help or if I wanted to talk, she'd listen.

Within six months, everyone in the unit knew I was in treatment. I was open and honest. Six to eight months later, something happened; and Jhenna told me that the person I was going to see didn't need to know I was in treatment. I was asked to do combat-related training. I thought I had to explain to him why I wasn't going to be participating and couldn't help. I think she told him I wouldn't be there.

During my next visit with the psychologist, I said that very story. I then told her that I just realized that I was to be open and honest with the care providers, not everyone. Too late now? The psychologist started laughing. I was laughing too. I had not laughed like that in a very long time.

I was embarrassed being in treatment and felt useless as a Soldier and a person. I didn't leave the house for nearly six months unless I had to go to the grocery store, which I did as soon as they opened with only a very few other shoppers. I was out of the store in under five minutes and back home for another week.

Because of that honesty, I had more support than I could imagine. Many of the Soldiers would have private conversations with me as I told them what it was like—the emotions, the hard work. Several later came and told me that they got into a program. Because I explained during our chats that there is no reason to feel embarrassed. I ask questions like, "Are you embarrassed when you ask for help moving a heavy object?" "Are you embarrassed when you don't know how to do something and ask for help?" It's all the same. Asking for help is just that.

Several who have been in treatment for years would then talk to me, and they felt the same way. They tell me not to worry, when you look back, you're going to laugh at how crazy your thinking was back then. Then they'd tell me of their crazy thoughts, and we could laugh. They were right, I do laugh. I'm laughing now telling this story to you, and we may never have met. If my being open and honest helps one person "have a chance to be happy, a chance to have friends, a chance to be loved," then I'm happy.

"Everyone gets angry sometimes, as long as it's not all the time, then you're good."

This was just a couple of months ago. I'd quit drinking in November 2023, never to drink again. I promised Jhenna, and it was easy. I used a book called *Quit Drinking Without Willpower* by Allen Carr. He also has one for stopping smoking, as he was a chain smoker; it was his first, and that was around 1983.

Then in April 2024, I got angry, which turned to rage, and I started drinking again. I had to tell Jhenna what I did because I told her I would. That's when she texted the above statement. There was a lot more to it. She said, "If you know what happened or caused it... I do, always anger. When that happened, I beat myself up as usual and got worse. The "Don't dwell on it" would have worked here. I didn't have the techniques two months ago that I have now and began implementing and will soon share with you. It seems like teams from both deployments where I served as the noncommissioned officer in charge (NCOIC) in my sections are all in treatment of some type for anger issues. Anger must be huge.

Now that I've implemented the techniques, two weeks later, I am not drinking anymore. I have realized that anger doesn't go away if it is left on its own. It sits hidden, waiting to resurface, when you least expect it. Dormant, patient, and getting stronger. Something happens, you're in an argument, and someone always seems to come up with a memory from the past and throws it in your face. Or someone does something that brings up that memory, and the fight ensues. Probably never happens to any of you, but for me, that's my sharpest sword. It doesn't help me at all. Now that I am aware of my tactics, I am working on it. This could be labeled as one of the deadly sins in a relationship, like generalizations such as *always* and *never*. That sparks anger in me fast. The "You never listen to me" response causes me to shut down. Sooner or later, tension gets high; and anyone or anything could set it off, even if it's not related. Then I'm just looking for a fight.

I learned about these triggers (button pushers) through being in treatment. Trying to get someone in treatment while unknowingly pushing their buttons probably won't work for treatment. How could it? Seems like that is poking a bear to make it go away. Sometimes it may work, but I'm thinking if you poke the bear for too long, it'll get angry. I'm trying to imagine the bear saying, "Fine! I'll go!" It's easier for me to imagine the bear saying, "That's not going to happen!" Keep poking, and you're probably going to be lunch.

Because I am in treatment, I become more aware of my triggers. This has been critical in learning not to be angry all the time and learning to find peace. It's taken over three years to get here with the tools I was using in the past. As you become aware of your triggers, you'll be able to address them and minimize or neutralize them. That has a lot of benefits in relationships of all kinds. We will cover some of what I've done to neutralize triggers later. Fortunately for me, with a hair-trigger anger response that has been forged over years of military service and even childhood, this is the one I worked the hardest to find a way to change. I don't think that the situation that causes anger needs to be changed in all cases. What must change is the way we respond.

"Don't worry about hurting. Everybody hurts. We can wallow in it or accept it, feel it, and move on. You can do that. I have faith in you."

In early treatment, I hurt all the time. It was a miserable eight months of my life. That was the hardest time for me. It is still hard some days, but the days are days, not months, not years. I work harder on the days that I hurt, using the tools that follow, because I didn't want to feel that pain. I had a huge support team of friends; all of them have PTSD. Two I deployed with as their noncommissioned officer in charge (NCOIC). One of the two that I deployed with served in Vietnam. It was probably one of the worst deployments, so it was sad to hear that when they returned home, they weren't treated well. And in those days, no one talked about mental health. It was always, "Suck it up!"

To me, "feel it and move on" took forever to learn to do, and I still struggle with it depending on the situation. My record for moving on is fifteen minutes, the fastest I ever moved on, and that was after more than two years of treatment. My norm seems to be three days. The goal is ten seconds or less. Life is too short to waste any time feeling down or hurting all the time. My shrink said, "You are too hard on yourself. You have to learn to stop beating yourself up." Not an easy thing, which is why I am still in treatment. In the first days of treatment, I thought everything would be over and done with after a couple of visits. I believed that because I wasn't better by then, I would never get better. That's when I put together a plan to leave this world. Fortunately, my chaplain at the time, my friend now, noticed something, and we talked for thirty minutes in the hallway. When things got deeper, we talked in his office for three hours. He was able to share a tool with me that I later pursued with my therapist called eye movement desensitization and reprocessing (EMDR). I explain this later in this book, as well as how I do it. It's a technique that was studied for more than two decades working with trauma patients.

"Don't think about what could go wrong. Think about what might go right!"

This quote from Jhenna reminded me of Earl Nightingale in his audio program, first recorded on an album called *The Strangest Secret*. In that recording, which I listened to over thirty years ago, he says that *The Strangest Secret* can be boiled down to only six words: "We become what we think about." I must have been too immature to understand it then. Maybe it sounded too simple. It made sense to me only after Jhenna's quote above. Jhenna always appeared to me to have everything together. I looked up to her. I did see her get angry once as I was giving her a ride. It only lasted maybe a minute. Then she apologized, and it was over. I thought, *Man, I wish I could get over stuff that fast.* I never told her that, of course. I never told her that I looked up to her. The Soldiers and friends that I have and work with on their PTSD challenges know Jhenna through me and have told me that I was lucky to have her in my life. Then they followed it up by saying that they were blessed by me because I was blessed by her. They are correct. Fortunately, to date, Jhenna hasn't asked me not to contact her anymore. I lean on her so much. I think just wondering if she will one day ask me not to reach out to her anymore causes me problems. That would fall under, "Don't think about what could go wrong. Think about what might go right!" It should be clear to you, the reader, by now that I still have a lot of work to do, and I can promise you that it is worth it.

"It's normal to have setbacks. Don't dwell on it, move forward, and you'll be at peace."

Some days, it seems I take a step forward and two backward. Jhenna reminded me to move forward. It was just like on missions. In the movie *We Were Soldiers*, with Mel Gibson, one of the Soldiers was calling in the bombing strike and made a mistake that caused a bomb to be dropped on friendly forces. I don't remember what Mel's character said to the Soldier, but it was pretty much what Jhenna said to me—to not dwell on it, but keep moving forward. This I have found to be critical. I also learned that as long as I keep moving forward, I don't dwell on it. When I stop focusing on moving forward, that is when I beat myself up. I am reminded of a blowout I had on the interstate in my car. I didn't stand around staring (dwelling) at the flat tire and pitching a fit or cussing myself out. I got the spare and changed it, then got back on the road. The physical stuff seems so much easier to go beyond than the mental stuff. The truth is, I've changed many flat tires. It's second nature to me. I have thirty years of practice changing tires. I don't have that many years of experience in getting mentally healthy. This would be a great place to give ourselves some credit that we are still working to get better. We don't know how much time it will take because we are all different and have different responsibilities as well as time constraints. My friend Kyle once said, "PTSD is not for the faint of heart." Truer words can't be spoken concerning PTSD. PTSD affects those of us who care about us as well. The more the folks around us understand that we are not thinking like mentally healthy people, the more they can help us get better. Cindy, my wife, now waits for me to pick a seat in a restaurant before she sits down. She knows I still watch the entrances and exits. She knows I constantly scan the crowd. It took me a long time to go out to eat without my wife begging me for months. Even now, she has to ask me a week or two in advance so that I can mentally prepare myself.

"Don't feel bad about falling off the horse. That can happen from time to time, but as long as you recognize how you got there and how to avoid it again, you're in good hands."

This was what Jhenna told me after four months of not drinking, then I had a very bad day and started drinking again. PTSD and drinking seem to be common. Unfortunately, it makes almost everything more difficult. Allen Carr wrote *Quit Drinking the Easy Way*. It's the book that I millions of others have used to quit drinking. Allen Carr has seminars that last about five hours, and at the end, if you don't quit drinking, he gives a full refund. The audiobook is what I used in my car for months. He also has *Quit*

Smoking the Easy Way. I saved a lot of money when I didn't drink.

I also noticed that I slept better, so my mood was better, which made me less argumentative. Lack of sleep is the worst thing for PTSD. Your body can't repair itself, and your mind doesn't have time to process.

"Very brave move to stop drinking. It will improve your life whether you believe it now!"

Jhenna always encourages everyone to do better. She was and continues to encourage me with her words of wisdom.

"Just breathe, and you'll be fine."
"Don't worry so much. Everything is fine, and you're doing well. Keep looking toward a happy future and manifest the happiness you seek. It will come."

This quote is one of the ones that drove me forward. This is the one that I believed and knew I had to find a way to beat PTSD. It took a few years, but as Jhenna said, "Keep looking toward a happy future." This is crucial to keeping a positive mental attitude.

I hope that this section illustrated how text messages aren't received the same by someone without mental health challenges. We think differently, and no matter how hard we try, we react differently. Some drink more than usual. In my case, I became angry and combative verbally, defensive. Jhenna understood a lot about mental trauma.

Texting lacks one very important part of communication: feedback. Without feedback, there is no communication. I found that the more text messages I received, the angrier I got with myself because I didn't understand the message. That led me to shutting down and becoming angry with myself. That's more anger and less understanding. Many times, I was told, "Don't worry about it, I'll find someone else to do what I asked." That made things worse for me and the folks around me. Before PTSD, I was a good Soldier. Some leaders that I deployed with said they didn't believe there was a finer NCO. After PTSD, I thought I was a substandard Soldier and that I was being treated that way. As I got better, I realized that I wasn't substandard, nor was I treated that way.

One of the things that PTSD caused me was confusion, misunderstanding things. I remember my first trip to New Jersey, and I was driving, trying to make a left-hand turn. I saw a sign that said, "All left-hand turns made from the right-hand lane." I ignored the sign because I couldn't imagine making a left-hand turn from the right-hand lane. After three or four of those signs, I decided to move to the right-hand lane to try to figure out how that was possible. That's when I discovered what is called a "jug handle." I had never heard of it before. The "jug handle" is a right-hand turn into a curve that takes you to a signal light so that you can make a left-hand turn. It does make turning around and U-turns safer for everyone on the road. I remember the first time I saw a roundabout and turned the wrong way in an eighteen-wheeler. That required the police to shut down the roundabout so that I could go around it the wrong way. PTSD is confusing because we must relearn to think correctly. That's why it is important for us to be patient with ourselves and avoid beating ourselves up. It's also important for those who love and care about us to be patient with us to give us a chance to learn to think correctly. It's frustrating to both parties involved. It is worth it to all parties. You'll see.

In the next section, we will get into the tools and how you can use them. They are the tools that I used to be able to beat PTSD and find peace. It's not magic, it's work, and I worked six to ten hours a day because I didn't want to be what I was and do what I did to people who cared about me. I just couldn't stop myself. I didn't have the tools. After two and a half years, I am still finding tools that help me become better.

PART 3

Tools

As you study and practice the tools in this section, you will find what works for you. They all worked for me, but eventually, I narrowed down the tools that I use. You will too.

The first tool is a device about the size of the newer flip phones or folding smartphones. It's called the Alpha-Stim device. Amazon has the M model, which is the one that I have, listed at $1,200.

I requested one from the VA, and due to being over 60 percent disabled, it didn't cost me anything. It relieves "pain, anxiety, and insomnia," as it states on the case it came in when I received it. Because I wasn't sleeping two or three days at a time, and when I did sleep it was only two or three hours a day, I used this device three times a day for an hour at a time. Anxiety affects your ability to sleep. Lack of sleep affects anxiety in a negative way.

I needed to sleep, and when I couldn't sleep, I would drink until I passed out. Drinking doesn't allow you to get good rest, but at the time, I was spiraling out of control, and my thinking was that turning off my brain was better than being awake. Seventy-two hours of a pounding in my chest or skipped heartbeats spiked my anxiety. After a week, maybe two, I started to sleep at least a little every other day, and then I was sleeping a little every day. I wasn't able to work because I didn't get out of bed every day and was too tired to think straight. As a former truck driver, I learned that fatigue driving carries the same number of points on your driving record as drunk driving. The reason being that fatigue has many of the characteristics of being drunk. Poor judgment is a big factor in both. You may not be able to use the device as often as I did because your responsibilities are likely different than mine. Not working, I had no responsibilities.

Moving on, in the book *The Body Keeps the Score*, written by Bessel van der Kolk, the author talks about four things that have been studied that work well for trauma:

- Acupuncture
- Massage
- Yoga
- Eye movement desensitization and reprocessing (EMDR)

They are listed in order of effectiveness. I didn't try acupuncture. I am a certified G-Jo acupressure practitioner, which is basically the same but without the needles.

Massage, on the other hand, I did try. What I found was that human touch does wonders for the mind and relaxation. Because Jhenna told me to be open and honest, and at first, I thought she meant to tell everyone, which I did, I began to have many people throughout the day hugging me and telling me everything was going to be okay. I found that as comforting and relaxing as a full-body massage. In fact, for me, it helped more than a full-body massage. You might think that should have been obvious because when babies cry, what do we do? We pick up the baby and comfort it, and usually, the baby settles down.

Yoga was one of my personal favorites. I was doing yoga four days a week. Being a guy, I got a lot of sideways looks as if to say, "Dude! You do yoga? That's for girls!" It's not just for girls. What yoga does is connect the mind and the body in forms of poses. It gives your mind something to focus on other than your problems. Usually done in a peaceful setting, it was easy for me to let go of my problems. In fact, following a yoga session, then immediately going to see my therapist, all I did was talk about yoga and how peaceful it is. I told her I couldn't do sessions after yoga anymore because when nothing is bothering you, how can you talk about what's bothering you? We would schedule before yoga after that.

EMDR I also used, and it was amazingly fast. The first time I did this was with my therapist. It involves working on a trigger that causes you to have an emotional response such as anger, anxiety, sadness, or any other emotion due to the memory that came up caused by the trigger.

The process involves recalling something from the past that causes an unwanted emotional reaction in your body, such as a car crash. The therapist asks you to rate the level of the emotion it causes on a scale from 1 to 10; 1 being it doesn't bother you at all, and 10 being it's extremely bothersome. Then, as you are recalling the event, she'll have you move your eyes from left to right by either following her finger as she moves it, following moving lights, or in my case, she had me close my eyes and switch from left to right and back while holding in my hand a device that, when it pulsates, you look in the direction of the pulse, whether it be left or right, while she observes you. At some point, she will say stop, and you open your eyes. She might ask you what was going on at that moment because she notices a change in your face, breathing, or even skin color. She'll have you rate the level of the emotion again on the scale of 1–10 on how much that memory still bothers you. This process continues until the number continues to approach one. You may move on to something else if the number reaches a certain point and stays there. You may return to that trigger in your following session.

What I found is that I could do this by myself with a countdown timer that repeats every ten seconds, and now I can do it without a timer. It's important to open your eyes before you reevaluate to break the cycle. This also works better for me than "take a breath" because I notice that when I have an unwanted emotion, I close my eyes as if I can't see the memory, and I automatically take a breath because I am usually getting upset with myself for having that emotion come up because a trigger was fired.

The eye movement from left to right activates the memory recall and memory construct portion of how you process things in your mind. Usually, you look left to recall and right to construct. You may have seen movies where they mention this technique of telling when the person is telling the truth or not when being questioned by a law enforcement officer. I first heard of this when studying neurolinguistic programming.

EMDR was best explained that you are taking a memory from long-term memory to short-term memory, blurring the memory, then placing it back in long-term memory, thereby desensitizing the memory. It's hard to get emotional about a blurry photograph because you can't see the details.

Mindfulness is another tool that I use. I have found that when I'm not mindful, I slip up. Some folks may refer to this as living in the moment. This takes a lot of practice. I remember two times when I wasn't mindful. The first is when I stopped using tobacco. I used snuff for six months. I was at a truck stop and about to check out, I got distracted by another driver, and before I knew it, I had purchased snuff and put it in my mouth before I knew it.

The second time was similar, only it involved a beer. At a shrimp boil with family, someone brought me a beer while eating, and I opened it and had finished the beer, drank a second one before I realized it. I remember thinking, *Messed that up, so I'll have to start over tomorrow.*

This happens every time I forget to take a breath before I speak when I am in what I perceive as a confrontation. It's also the first thing I thought of when I started mental health treatment. It has been more than three and a half years since I started treatment with a therapist and only two and a half years since I started treatment with a psychologist. A point to be made here is that all therapists are not created equally. One of my good friends is in treatment, and when he told me nothing seemed to work, I told him to see someone else, and he could always go back to the current therapist. I did get a new therapist, and he told me it was like the difference between night and day. He is doing much better now.

Visualization and imagination are the next tools. You may have heard it said, "If you can imagine it, you can have it. If you can dream it, you can achieve it," or some other version of the same thing. I have mentioned Earl Nightingale's "We become what we think about." If you think about something long enough, it will happen because you'll get excited about it. That excitement is energy and is everything. This tool doesn't need any explaining. The quote in the dedication says it all. Moving on.

The next group of tools that I have been really focused on over the last two months was intentions, affirmations, and belief statements. These have really accelerated changes in me. Intention statements have been the most powerful for me, and let me tell you two stories that will without a doubt illustrate their power.

The first story came from a former commander (CO) of mine. He lives in Pensacola. He told me of a time when his electric bill was high, and he made the intention of lowering the electric bill. In his case, it may not have been a formal intention statement, yet he was taking action to make it happen. We talked about taking action earlier. He told me he had two daughters, and they always left lights on and other electrical things on, even when they weren't in the room or using them. He would often turn off the lights and other things that weren't being used and remind the girls that they needed to turn things off that weren't being used.

This went on for a while, and reminding them wasn't working, so he came up with another plan that he thought might help. He started telling them that if they didn't turn off the things they weren't using, and the lights were a big thing, they were going to start paying the electric bill. As you can imagine, this went on for a while, and it wasn't working either. With his intention and focus, he came up with another plan. He made them start paying the electric bill. This went on for a while as well. They were paying the electric bill and still leaving the lights on, which he didn't mind because they were paying the bill. This went on for a while, but something changed. Sometimes the lights were on, sometimes off. The girls began to beg him to pay the electric bill. He said no because the lights were still being left on sometimes. Then he noticed the lights were being turned off all the time. I don't know how long the girls begged him after the lights were always off when not in use, but it seems like a while. Finally, he was convinced that the lights were turned off all the time, so he agreed to pay the electric bill again and cautioned the girls that if he saw the lights on again, they would start paying the bill again. He never had that problem again.

The second story took place in the mountains of Afghanistan. The same CO, only he was the executive officer (XO) during this tour, was heading up a mountain in armored-up SUVs. In Afghanistan, he told the CO that I was his NCO, and the CO never questioned it. The XO never went anywhere without me. In fact, I was getting ready to deploy, and he told me that he would not allow me to deploy by myself, so he was going to deploy with me.

So back to the mountain. We were heading up the mountain, and the XO was my tactical commander (TC). I was always the driver, among other things, and we were so far up the mountain that the vehicles at the bottom looked like ants. At about that time, one of the vehicles blew out a radiator hose and overheated, coming to a stop. Now, in case you didn't know, the roads in Afghanistan are mostly unpaved, there are no guardrails to keep you from going over the side, and they are narrow two lanes, more like one and a half lanes.

The driver stepped out of the vehicle, walked to the front of the vehicle, and happened to look over the side of the mountain. Panic immediately set in, and he announced he was afraid of heights. The XO's intention was to get the vehicle down the mountain. With the engine not working, the power steering and power brakes wouldn't work, and these vehicles were heavy.

So all of us were standing around trying to figure out how to get the vehicle down. The vehicle happened to stop at a turnout, which is where if two vehicles approached each other, one had to go into the turnout, or neither could get through. With seven Soldiers pushing, moving forward and backward about five times, we finally got it turned around. So I volunteered to drive it down. A question was brought up about power steering and power brakes not working. The first one was easy. When the vehicle is rolling, steering is possible; it takes a bit more effort. What about brakes? That seemed simple to me, strap a vehicle to the rear, and that vehicle would be our brakes. It took some time to find enough straps to strap them securely, but we got it done. It was getting late, and the sun was going down. We were running out of time.

The final thing we needed to do was get a driver for the other vehicle and a TC for both, then everyone else would pile into the other vehicles just in case we went over the side. The XO volunteered to be my TC. I said, "Sir, I need someone I trust in the other vehicle, and that's you. You be on the radio, give me a radio man, and let's go!" I let the other driver know that we would be going down at no more than fifteen miles per hour because his brakes would burn up if we went any faster, and if either vehicle went over the side, we'd both go over. I'd tell my radio guy to slow down, he'd tell the other radio guy to slow down, and we'd go down that mountain in complete silence except for "Slow down" and "Slow down more." The switchbacks would be the scariest part of the trip, and the mountain was mostly switchbacks.

So we made it to the bottom of the mountain. One final step: get the vehicle to the forward operating base (FOB). I said, "That's the easy part. The engine is cool. I'll start it and drive as fast as I can so that if it overheats, I can coast the rest of the way. We will call the guards to open the gates and stand clear because we are coming in hot." And that is exactly what we did. The engine overheated, I put it in neutral, no brakes, and coasted into the gate, which starts uphill when you enter. We made it halfway before it stopped, and before it could start rolling backward, I slammed it into park. Mission accomplished, intention met.

There are many other stories I could tell, like the time I promised a lieutenant that I'd get his pay problem fixed and backpay paid in forty-five days or less. I could tell you how Cindy and I got married using a belief statement. There are so many. And this book tells the story of believing I would beat PTSD. There is no cure, but it is so much better living like I am now than I was when Jhenna told me I had to go, or it would be command mandated. I can tell you that if you don't believe it, it won't happen.

Intentions, affirmations, and belief statements ground rules: you must believe them. They are most powerful when you create your own. If they don't get you excited and bring a smile to your face, they need to be rewritten. If you aren't excited about your statements, you won't follow through. Following through daily, at three times a day, moving toward fifteen times a day, is a must to take root and grow. I believed I could beat PTSD, and I have been told by many friends and others that they are proud of me because some of them know that I had created a plan to leave this world prematurely. With their encouragement and their belief in me, I canceled the plan as I began to get better.

I'm guessing that most everyone has heard of affirmations. The way I learned them was they all start with "I am," followed by whatever it was that you desired. Always in the present like it existed. And it would happen. I just didn't believe what I was saying, and trust is my highest value. I wasn't inspired or passionate about what I was saying. Then I found a different way of writing affirmations that I could get passionate about. I wrote them as "I love the idea of…" or "I'm looking forward to…" I couldn't say, "I am free from mental health illness," and believe it. I say, "I am looking forward to [or "I love the idea of"] being free from mental health illness." That I got passionate about. That made me excited, and that drove me to work harder. In other words, to take massive action to get there.

I used belief statements, but they quickly turned into intention statements. When Jhenna said to me, "If you get mental health treatment, you'll have a chance to be happy, a chance to have friends, and a chance to be loved," I believed her because I trusted her. I can write a belief statement: "I believe that what Jhenna said is true." I wanted that. I worked my butt off to get that. I just don't write them. I believe that those of you that love someone with mental health issues and are supportive with choosing your statements as well as Jhenna did could get your loved one into mental health treatment. Not through nagging or constantly saying, "You need help," but by doing your belief statement as something like, "I believe my loved one will get the help he needs for his PTSD soon," your behavior will change and put the energy in motion that will cause the result. Because you are taking inspired action on what comes to mind. I didn't believe I could get better until after six to eight months of treatment. The only reason I kept going is because Jhenna believed, and I trusted her.

Now the intention statements really got me passionate. My statement is, "My intention is to beat PTSD and get mentally healthy." That turns me on. Another intention statement that I have is, "My intention is to find a way to beat PTSD and help others get mentally healthy." I've been doing that, but it wasn't enough. I changed the second part of my statement to, "and help as many people as humanly possible to become mentally healthy." One person can only do so much, but a book can reach millions in a year and millions more for centuries to come. You are reading that book. I didn't know anything about intention statements until recently. For me, they are amazing.

This book is being written because of something I said to Jhenna. I don't remember what she said. I remember my response to her was, "You should write a book called *The Jhenna* because I don't quote the Bible, but I can quote *The Jhenna*." She responded with something funny, and the idea was born. Then I acted. It wasn't easy to put my personal story and struggles out there like this, and it wasn't easy to write it. If it helps just one more person that I may not have been able to reach otherwise, then the struggle is worth it. I was at death's door two and a half years ago. I'm not anymore. I'm still moving forward. From three mental health sessions a week at the VA to once a month now. I found peace. I was angry all the time, and now maybe once a month, and that lasts anywhere from fifteen minutes to three days. Much better than three years to twenty years.

PART 4

Final Words

I believe that every one of you can beat PTSD and find peace.

I believe that every one of you who lives with or loves someone with PTSD can use the tools that I shared to help your loved one find peace.

My intention is that everyone who reads this book finds the help they need.

My intention is that everyone who reads this book understands that those with mental health or without mental issues work together to help each other heal.

I believe we all want to find peace.

I believe that we all want to be happy.

I believe that we all want to have wonderful people in our lives to love, and to be loved by.

I believe we are all stronger than we think and are stronger together.

My intention is that *The Jhenna* becomes part of the solution to mental health illness.

I look forward to everyone becoming mentally healthy.

I love the idea of everyone with PTSD working hard on themselves to get mentally healthy.

PART 5

Conclusion

Long before I was born, many wonderful folks lived and had goals and dreams. They created things like automobiles and airplanes. They had so many ideas that sounded crazy at the time that they were probably considered crazy. Yet they all took action to accomplish their goals and dreams. I am old enough to remember phones built into cars, then bag phones, which later became more portable but weighed about two pounds with the battery. They were expensive, and I knew only one or two people who had them. Today, many of us have cell phones and use them daily. The one thing that every one of the inventors did that most won't is that they took action to accomplish their goals and dreams. They focused on what they wanted. They didn't listen to the naysayers. They kept moving forward.

We must do the same thing. Act every day to get better. Put what we learn to use. Failure to act changes nothing. I once heard that the only place success comes before work is in the dictionary. That was as true then as it is today. Working to get mentally healthy is not easy. I wanted to give up every day. I felt like quitting every day. Some days, I stayed in bed. What I did right was I had a goal that I wanted so bad that I started to get out of bed every day. It was hard work learning to get out of bed every day. Something that I had done all my life became difficult. Then I got better at it. Then I had to learn to go out in public again—again, something I did most of my life. That was a lot harder than getting out of bed. So I worked at it. I didn't go on vacations, nor did I look forward to vacations. I'll be taking my third trip to Disney World within eight months. Talk about getting out of bed and going out in public? This was huge for me. And now I am enjoying the vacations that I take. Now I do get overwhelmed sometimes, so I go back to the hotel room and settle down, center myself, then I go out to the parks again. It took time.

Give yourself time, use the tools contained within this book. Some will work better than others for you. That's okay. Find your own tools. Do something! Do anything! If it doesn't work, *great*! You found something that didn't work for you. Keep moving forward. You can beat PTSD. Of course, you'll have bad days. Even infants have bad days. You know what the infants do already, they keep moving forward, and they don't dwell on anything.

Let me leave you with this from Matthew 7:7: "Ask, and it shall be given to you; seek, and ye shall find; knock, and it shall be opened unto you." It really is that simple. It only becomes difficult when we lose sight of our goal. My goal was simple: I wanted to make Jhenna proud of me, and I would stop at nothing to make that happen.

In writing this book, I had goals: to share with you my journey to beat PTSD by being open and honest, which is what Jhenna told me to be, in hopes that the tools I used would help you and yours. I started the journey with an exit strategy because I was hurting so badly that I didn't want to go on in this world, but I wanted to make Jhenna proud. I am grateful that she didn't give up on me. I am grateful that many others like her didn't give up on me. I know that what is in this book works because I did it. Have faith that you can too. I have faith in you. Without faith, nothing changes; without faith, there can't be dreams. If you don't have faith that you can win the battle of mental health, find someone who believes in you and use their faith for as long as it takes to build your own faith. Pat yourself on the back for the small battles until you win the war. Give yourself credit for at least reading this book. It may be the starting point that you need. And always remember, "Ask, and it shall be given to you; seek, and ye shall find; knock, and it shall be opened unto you." If you ever had a child who wanted some ice cream, you know they never stop asking until they get what they want, even if it takes a week or a month. The children get creative in their ways to ask for that ice cream. And they never give up. Don't give up.